MW01028228

Advance praise for *Prayers and Blessings for Healthcare Workers*

"In these pages you will encounter restorative, life-giving words that speak to the commonalities of our journeys, and you will find affinity in their beautiful reminders of love's perseverance. A much-needed exhale for the world."

—JOHN PAVLOVITZ,
author of *A Bigger Table*

"This beautiful and inspiring collection of prayers and blessings provides words for those of us who were left speechless by the pandemic. It is a must-read for anyone who wishes to mark this difficult moment in history with light and hope."

—AMANDA HELD OPELT,
writer, musician

Prayers
and
Blessings
for
Healthcare
Workers

Prayers
and
Blessings
for
Healthcare
Workers

Edited by
Mandy Mizelle

 Morehouse Publishing
NEW YORK

Morehouse Publishing, 19 East 34th Street, New York, NY 10016

Morehouse Publishing is an imprint of Church Publishing Incorporated.

Cover design by Jennifer Kopec, 2Pug Design
Typeset by Progressive Publishing Services

Library of Congress Cataloging-in-Publication Data

Names: Mizelle, Mandy, editor.
Title: Prayers and blessings for healthcare workers / Mandy Mizelle.
Description: New York, NY : Morehouse Publishing, [2021]
Identifiers: LCCN 2021016129 (print) | LCCN 2021016130 (ebook) | ISBN
    9781640654808 (hardcover) | ISBN 9781640654815 (epub)
Subjects: LCSH: Caregivers—Prayers and devotions. | Medical
    personnel—Prayers and devotions.
Classification: LCC BV4910.9 .P73 2021 (print) | LCC BV4910.9 (ebook) |
    DDC 242/.68—dc23
LC record available at https://lccn.loc.gov/2021016129
LC ebook record available at https://lccn.loc.gov/2021016130

For the hands, feet, hearts, and breath of frontline healthcare workers who have held and steadied and cared for and—quite literally—breathed into us this past year, even when it was uncertain and dangerous for them to do so.

For you.

Contents

For Your Grounding

For Your Hands

For Your Heart

For Your Breath

For Your Becoming

Introduction

Last year, six months into a worldwide pandemic, I became a Decedent Care chaplain.

If you don't know what Decedent Care means, you're in good company. Many people aren't sure what it means or how to pronounce it, including colleagues in my hospital and lots of folks who regularly call our office asking for *Decadent* Care. *Decadent,* you may remember from the Before Times, means self-indulgent or luxurious. I don't know exactly what a Decadent Care department would do—I'm imagining providing chocolate and wine and lotion, plush bath robes instead of ill-fitting paper gowns—but we could certainly use such a department after the past year.

Decedent, on the other hand, means a person who has died. A more familiar definition these days. At the time of my writing this, there have been nearly three million decedents worldwide due to COVID-19. As a Decedent Care chaplain in the time of Covid, most mornings I am in the morgue before I have had a cup of coffee. If that doesn't scream "pandemic,"

I don't know what does. Often, I am there to place a death certificate with a body before a funeral home or cremation service arrives to pick up and continue post-mortem care. More importantly (to me), I am there to acknowledge and honor the bodies of these particular persons who have died. *Passed. Transitioned.* Or, as hospitals so eloquently put it: *expired.* A word conjuring meanings of *giving out* that may resonate with you, at the front of whatever lines, plural, on which you work and live—not only as healthcare worker, but as healthcare needer, parent, partner, adult child, sibling, friend . . . *humaning* through these long days and months. Years?

While my own faith tradition and spirituality tell me that after death, a person's essence—spirit, soul—is no longer bound by skin and bone, it is important to me to honor the sacred and fragile body, made of dust and divinity, with which that person moved through and inhabited this sacred and fragile, dusty and divine world. Squatting on my heels at the foot of each gurney, I offer a prayer or blessing, depending on what I know of the person's religious or spiritual orientation, for the body before me, the spirit that inhabited it, the people and places it touched, the ones it loved.

Afterwards, as I make my way back upstairs to the land of the living and coffee-drinking, I silently continue acknowledging and honoring all kinds of bodies that I meet, from the currently prescribed distance: bodies that are suffering, bodies that are healing, bodies that are in recovery and remission. Bodies that are growing, bodies that are changing, bodies that are in between. Bodies that are broken, bodies that are hurting, bodies that are tired—of wearing masks, of sanitizing, of staying six feet apart. Bodies that are caring, bodies that are tending, bodies that are saving. Bodies that are trying. Bodies that are failing. Bodies that are.

Bodies like yours. Bodies like mine.

Whatever we experience, behold, believe, value, it happens through—and, to some extent, because of—our bodies. And what a brutal year it has been for our bodies. Our bodies have gone without hugs and handshakes and haircuts. Without enough touch. Without enough sleep. Without enough energy. Without enough resources—masks, beds, ventilators, vaccines, childcare, paychecks, sick time, time off, time with anyone who doesn't live in our house . . .

This collection of prayers, blessings, meditations, and poems has been written and put together with your body in mind—your essential and exhausted body, your sacred and fragile body made of dust and divinity, that has been on the frontlines of a more than yearlong pandemic. More accurately, syndemic, with co-occuring crises of COVID-19 and systemic racism here in the United States, devastating our individual and collective bodies, minds, spirits. The words held within these pages, the words you now hold in your hands, are offered by spiritual, mental, and emotional care providers on the frontlines and in the trenches alongside you, both in and beyond hospital rooms. They come from voices who have cared for dying friends and family members as they have cared for dying patients. Who have welcomed a beloved baby born with medical complexities during an extraordinarily medically and humanly complex year. Who have moved and started over, been out of work and overworked, not known if they had enough to give.

These prayers and blessings have been gathered up into a series of sections offered as balm to the places in your body and being likely in need of comfort and courage:

your *grounding*, for rest and reconnection for tired feet
    and soul
your *hands*, for receiving peace and releasing the heaviness
you have held,
your *heart*, for compassion and affirmation,
your *breath*, for pause and re-creation,
your *becoming*, for all that is yet to appear and blossom . . .

May the words on these pages, and the hearts of all who offer them, be a source of healing and of hope to you.

— Rev. Mandy Mizelle

April 2021

A Note about
Language and Editing

As a multi-faith project, this book embraces and celebrates a wide spectrum of spiritual traditions and orientations from contributors as well as readers of the collection. Each prayer and blessing, meditation and poem is offered authentically, wholeheartedly, from the writer's own spiritual or religious grounding while also making room for resonance among readers from other traditions and perspectives. With that in mind, there were times when the original words of a prayer or blessing were slightly adapted to more expansive language, while honoring the spirit of the piece. Whatever your spiritual language or practices, I hope this book feels inviting, with pages that connect with what is sacred and meaningful to you.

This collection also embraces and celebrates each writer's unique voice and creative license. In places, variation in capitalization and punctuation is intentional, reflecting the subject or spirit of the piece. Lines may evoke the act of breathing, for example, or signify the writer's own sense of urgency and outpouring of emotion. As you read, notice what speaks to you in the words and characters, spaces and shapes on the page.

For Your Grounding

Be still and know
        who
that ~~where~~ you were,
    are,
        will be,
          is holy.

Take off your shoes
    and hear the Ground
      calling.

"Rest."

                    — Rev. Mandy Mizelle

Front and Center

Let me sing another song
up to the front lines today.

To a pastor in Connecticut
who's reaching out to touch
the quivering hand—through
latex gloves—of a parishioner,
who had to watch a daughter die
behind glass, in a tangle of tubes,
to offer no prayer through a mask,
since no prayer would do. Not now.

To the nurse up in Minneapolis, who
had Covid herself, and felt the death
in its grip, but who now has to turn
to a family outside a window, down
on the sidewalk, to signal with eyes
that the end has come, and is gone.

To a doctor in North Carolina who
never thought, as the acting chief
of surgery, that she would long
for the days of broken bones
and knee replacements.

To a first responder who
bursts into dangerous air
every time a call comes in.

To a caregiver whose mind
is not allowed any days off,
who counts pills in her sleep,
worries if she cleaned the mail
and cans of soup from the store
enough to be safe, and wonders if,
when her time comes, she'll receive
the same kindness and consideration.

To a mental health worker in Austin
who is applying a tourniquet, best
he can, to the collective psyche
of a species, but knows the sheer
level of loss that's already occurred
will alter the shape of a generation.

We do not know all that you are
going through, but we do have
an idea where we wouldn't be
without the work you've done.

                                                    — *Nathan Brown*

A Love Song to All the Helpers

There will always be more pain than fits in your arms.

There will always be longing, incompleteness.

Let it all be real, and staggering,

And there is also the way that every day

People wake up and walk into

Difficult rooms,

Give care without expecting return,

Believe in a thousand things greater than themselves.

And there is also the way that every day,

People take pain and memory, and let it open them

To more empathy,

To the silence that can just be held.

And there is also you,

And this present moment,

And your reply.

— *Rev. Laura Martin*

Prayer for a New Day

God of this never seen before day
God of this new chance to live
God of this new story unfolding
We thank You for the gift of today
We thank You for waking us up
We thank You for giving us breath
We ask You to guide our way
We ask You to inspire our thoughts
We ask You to speak truth into our words
We ask You to empower our actions
We pray for grace to listen
We pray for peace to be still
We pray for mercy to let go
We pray for love to ground us
Amen

— Rev. Dr. Sarah Griffith Lund

A Prayer Before Commencing a Shift

I offer my praises to You, Adonai our God, Spirit of the Universe, who formed my body with wisdom and graciously endowed it with Your Spirit. I pray that as I go about my sacred work, I use my talents and gifts to extend Your compassion to those who are ill and in pain in this hospital.

I approach my work today in a time of uncertainty and fear. My body, which You formed with wisdom, has many strengths; I am grateful for my health and wellbeing. Yet I am acutely aware of its vulnerabilities. As I don this PPE, I am humbled by its ability to protect me; may I be ever mindful to use it effectively and preserve my health.

May I continue to feel Your Presence accompanying me each step of the day. May it be Your will that I be kept in safety and health.

My praises to You, Adonai, Guardian of Your people and Source of Health.

— Rabbi Brian T. Nelson

Blessing for Donning and Doffing

While this blessing was written with clinical colleagues in mind, it can be adapted to apply to whatever your own context, circumstance, and activities are at the moment. For example, instead of offering these words while placing on gloves, you can do so while scrubbing dishes, lacing up running shoes, pulling weeds, correcting middle school math problems, playing cards with your partner, logging on for a Zoom call, sewing masks for an elderly neighbor, etc. In short, please edit the blessing below so that it can be useful in your life. Even better, if you know someone who may need a blessing—an extra dose of spiritual TLC— take a quiet moment and offer these words up on that person's behalf, trusting that in the mystery of our human connection, it will be felt.

Personal protective equipment (PPE) protects your body from exposure to a virus while you care for vulnerable patients. Protecting your mind and spirit is important while you work, too. You are valued and special; your skills are needed and appreciated. As you serve to help others heal, your whole self is worthy of being healthy and strong, too. As you like, incorporate the meditative words below into your practice as you don and doff PPE. These blessings are from no particular spiritual tradition and are written on purpose with courageous clinicians—like you—in mind.

Blessing for Donning

As you don each piece of your gear, take deep, grounding breaths and read—or remember—the words below. You can also ask a colleague to read them aloud as you move through each step.

1. (Placing on gloves) *May my hands be gentle and caring*

2. (Slipping arms through the gown sleeves) *May my arms be sturdy and strong*

3. (Tying all of the ties on the gown) *May my body be grounded in service*

4. (Securing respirator/face mask) *May my words offer encouragement*

5. (Putting on face shield or goggles) *May I see a person before me and not just a patient*

6. (Entering patient room) *May this encounter be safe and healing for all*

Blessing for Doffing

As you doff each piece of your gear, take deep, grounding breaths and read, remember, or have read to you these words:

1. (Removing and disposing of gloves) *May what I offered be enough*

2. (Untying and disposing of gown) *May I release all that weighs me down and let it go*

3. (Exiting patient room) *May I move on with clarity and purpose*

4. (Performing hand hygiene) *May I feel fresh and clean and safe*

5. (Removing face shield or goggles) *May I see myself and others through a lens of compassion*

6. (Removing respirator/face mask) *May I inhale gratitude and exhale peace*

— Rev. Hadley Kifner

For Those Who Walk in the Footsteps

Do you ever wonder how Jesus felt

      after a long day healing lepers and raising the dead?

Do you ever wonder if he was bone-tired,

      whether you could look at his face and know

      he's thinking,

            "Could I have done something else or

            something more?"

Did he ask himself whether he would be able to go back

for another day

      of a hundred frightened faces,

         another hundred pleas for help,

            and a thousand unanswered

            questions?

In these moments when caregivers

      are full of wondering,

we lift them up.

In these days and weeks of fatigue and frustration,

      we give thanks that they go back for another day.

In these lingering months of confusion
      as to what this virus might do next,
we pray for their enduring strength.

Thanks be to our God
      who became incarnate in Jesus of Nazareth
        and showed us how to walk through
        the throngs
          of those who need healing.

Thanks be for those who walk in his footsteps—
      those who give aid and comfort to the sick.
Amen and Amen.

— Rev. Paula A. Wells

For Parents Who Leave Their Children at Home to Care for Others and You Feel as Though You Are the Cobbler and Your Children Have No Shoes

May your children be formed by the knowledge that the work you do makes a difference in the world, your community, and their own lives.

May you know that the time invested in this season of hurt and deep grief will be redeemed in future seasons of healing and peace.

May you have a good cry every now and then.

May you connect with counselors and friends who shepherd your story and hear your sorrows.

May you know the comfort of a plate full of vegetables or a bowl full of ice cream, each at the right time.

May your work remain at the threshold of your front door and not follow you inside.

May you notice nature on your commute: a bird, an insect, a ray of sunshine.

May your children be well cared for by surrogates when you are apart.

May you know how deeply your patients and children appreciate you, even as they may not be able to speak their gratitude with words.

May you be free of the nagging sense of guilt that you're always leaving somebody behind.

May you know the power of a strong cup of coffee, a soft pair of pajamas, a hot shower.

May you let go of the things "the other parents" can attend to that you cannot.

May you embrace the shortcuts that make your busy life easier—takeout, delivery, and one-day shipping.

May you rest well and fully, that you might have the strength to wake up and do it all again tomorrow.

May all of these things and more be yours,

Amen and Amen.

— *Rev. Traci Smith*

Prayer for Those Who Step into the Mess

God who walked among us and sometimes mixed mud and spit to heal or healed by words alone: Bless those who step into the mess when the rest of us keep our distance. Guard their health so that they may continue to do your work in this world. Inspire us to follow their lead, to heal with touch or words. We ask this in your own holy name. Amen.

— *Rev. Elizabeth Felicetti*

Blessing in a Pandemic

We go to the Gospels
Looking for Real Jesus
Incarnate God among us.

What did Jesus say?
Love God and
Each other.

What did Jesus do?
Brought wholeness—
True Shalom.

Healed a woman,
The mother
Of Peter's wife,

And lepers, whom
He did not fear
To touch.

Healed a servant,
A paralytic, one
Born blind.

They came to Him
Alone, or as part
Of a crowd

He turned away
No one, worthy,
Unworthy alike,

All were healed
By His word
Or His touch.

Today we bless
Those who have
Followed Him

Into ERs and ICUs,
Crowded rooms filled
With pain and distress,

Facing deadly
Contagion, to be
With those who suffer.

Wiping away sweat,
Soothing fears, giving
ALL of themselves.

Nurses, doctors, those
Who tend or clean, bring
Kindness to the darkness.

Blessed are those who heal,
For they shall be honored
On earth and in heaven.

Blessed are those who
Comfort, for they shall be
Held in the arms of God.

— Rev. Ruth McMeekin Skjerseth

For Those Who Keep the Ceiling From Falling In and Floors From Falling Out

God who Created and tends to Creation,
thank you for all who keep these buildings
and rooms and halls running.
Thank you for their skill to know how to fix the AC
when it breaks or who to call to fix the elevators.
Thank you for their patience with us when we try to
explain what we need, but really have no idea what
we're talking about; we just know it needs to be fixed.
Thank you for their faithfulness,
for all they do to keep the ceiling from falling on us
and the floors from falling out from under us.
Thank you for their kindness and their commitment.
Without them, no patient would get the care they need
to hope and to heal.
Merciful and Gracious God, keep all our facilities teams
safe in the palm of your hand.
May they know they are valued and appreciated.
Give them the strength and wisdom they need to
carry on even when they are overwhelmed
and feel under-appreciated.

May they know they are heroes to us
and to the patients in our care
whether we realize it or not.
All this we pray in your precious and holy name,
Amen.

— Rev. Sonya Gravlee

A Blessing for Caregivers

Blessed are you,

who care for people:

You, helping professionals in education, social work, and activism.

You, healthcare providers and humanitarian aid workers,

people from all walks of life, in vital caretaking roles.

Blessed are you,

when you feel tired and depleted,

when your own health and wellbeing is at stake,

when the burden and overwhelm exceed your reserves

and affect your ability to be present at home or at work.

Blessed are you,

when you seek balance in your dedication to serving others,

when you navigate the stress to avoid burnout,

when you consider your own health and wellbeing,

when you ask for what you need,

when you advocate for yourself and

when you make some choices for sustainability and joy.

Blessed are you,
as you make time to recharge physically,
mentally, and spiritually
so that you show up grounded and present,
rested and balanced,
to resume your life-giving work from a place of fullness.

May you know that you are loved.
May you know that you are blessed.
May you know that God is with you
in the all of it. Amen.

— *Rev. Kathy Bozzuti-Jones*

Prayer for Leaning

We are leaning, Lord. In these days of illness and worldwide fear, we feel like we're all going to fall down. We find comfort in the words of the old hymn that calls us to lean on your everlasting arms. And yet we remain afraid.

We pray today for ourselves—and we pray for everyone, because we are all in this together. Please make yourself known in the midst of us and pour out your Spirit of peace upon us. Grant us the courage to believe that we indeed are safe and secure from all alarms.

This seems to be an impossible prayer in these days, Lord. Help our unbelief.

We pray for your divine guidance for the things that are beyond our control, the things we cannot change. We pray for world leaders—and especially for our own national, state, and local leaders—to humble themselves and be guided by reason rather than ego. We pray for all those around us who seem so eager to exchange the hard truth for a more pleasant lie that has the power to kill thousands. We cannot control the attitudes and behaviors of others, but we pray that all people everywhere might be filled with your wisdom from on high and know how to live as community in these days.

We pray, especially today, for those who serve on the front lines of care—for the custodians who clean hospital rooms and grocery stores for minimum wage, for the lab technicians who handle precious test samples with urgency, for the doctors and nurses and chaplains who endanger themselves every hour in the quest to be agents of healing. Protect them all and the many others who give of themselves freely in these days.

We pray for parents and teachers and children who are adapting to new ways of learning. We pray for patience and wisdom and endurance through the unseen stressors of each day. And we pray for the safety of all who live in close confinement today and are subject to outbursts of rage and frustration. Pour out your Spirit of peace, we pray.

Hear our prayers, Lord, offered today with heavy hearts because of the state of our world, your world. Grant us wisdom and courage for the living of these days. Leaning into your grace and peace, we pray. Amen.

— *Rev. Mark Wingfield*

A Prayer for All During Coronavirus

Creator God,
we as a community, as a nation, as a world,
are in chaotic, ever-scrambling disarray.

One microscopic virus
is completely upending our sense of normalcy,
our comfortable, known patterns of behavior,
our sense of available daily resources,
our ability to interact with closeness and touch without fear.

We are people of faith, social beings
called by You to communicate kindness,
honesty, faith, hope, and love . . .
yet we now have a new rule of six feet of separation
from those we earnestly desire to support,
to listen to, to advocate for, to journey with.

Walk with us, God,
when we reactively retreat into our internal primal fears of
becoming infected,
of being deprived of survival substances,
of being isolated from family and much-needed fellow travelers.
Cleanse us, heal us, gift us with gratitude.

Grant us the security of inner centeredness—
seeing beyond the obvious chaos
so that we can be a non-anxious presence
with ourselves,
just as we long to be with our neighbors and world.

Hear our prayer, Creator God.

          Amen

— Dr. Virgil Fry

Reminders

- The weight of the world is not my burden to carry
- My self-care is not selfish or indulgent
- My joy is also what the world needs
- I have everything I need to love myself
- My body is worthy of some extra attention and gentleness
- I can do hard things and feel hard feelings
- My body is beautiful, capable, and resilient—even when it hurts
- I can always pause for a moment of stillness and silence
- Rest—deep, restorative rest—is sacred work
- Beauty is everywhere, if we have eyes soft enough to see it
- The space between two people is holy
- The peace I create in the world will come back to me
- I am not alone; I belong to the great family of all things
- The world is more lovely and whole with me in it

— Rev. Keith A. Menhinick

For Your Hands

What if
the lines on your hands mark
all you have loved,

all you have
                lost,

all you have tried
and
failed

and tried
again—

the point to touch every surface
of this world,

a wide-eyed toddler in Gods backseat,

fingerprints
        all over

            everything?

                — Rev. Mandy Mizelle

A Prayer for the Young Man (Who Makes Not Much an Hour for Hazardous Duty)

There he is
the first person
the very first one
to share the air
with patients incoming
aware of this invisible thing
that cannot be corralled
a part of our earth now
or always has been
he wears a mask
and so do we
I've seen him twice
he's the first one, God
did I say that already
his service is simple
he helps drivers
and passengers
mostly strangers
but for sure
some repeat customers
the young man

who parks their cars
at the clinic
yes, God
that healthcare worker
the one who is in front
of the front line
he neither treats
nor diagnoses
he parks
their cars
all day
every day
the sick and lame
not lowered down
through a hole in the roof
but driving in
to place their car
which when you add an "e"
becomes care
with his hands
he wipes down the steering wheel
perfunctory
but duty bound
bless him
and please protect him
how great thou art

he is all day
earning his wage
the first to say hello
and inhabit the air
in front of the front line
don't forget him
God
of course you wouldn't
because you just reminded me
not to.
Amen.

— Rev. Kevin M. Roberts

Blessing for Your Hands

Blessed are these hands that embrace strangers with gentleness and patience, nurture and compassion.

Blessed are these hands that change diapers, titrate medicines, flush boluses, run chemo, and offer ice chips.

Blessed are these hands that are dry and chapped from frequent washing, cramped and clenched from stress.

Blessed are these hands that pass on the tradition of nursing from one generation to the next—training, teaching, and encouraging.

Blessed are these hands that type emails, return phone calls, complete LMS trainings online, and send pages.

Blessed are these hands that know suffering and healing, death and recovery.

Blessed are these hands that love, heal, and touch—not just the body but the spirit, too.

Blessed are these hands that care for others outside of this unit and beyond this hospital, encouraging their own families and loved ones.

Blessed are these hands that are strong and sturdy, humble and human.

Blessed are these hands.

Blessed are your hands.

Amen.

— Rev. Hadley Kifner

A Tuesday Afternoon in 2020

Is my mask sealed fully?
I breathe out with force
and suck in air,
to check.
Is it a little wet from my spit from talking?
Or my nose that keeps running?
Or my sweat?
Did I wash my hands long enough?
Did I stay too long in the room?
Will I bring the virus to the next vulnerable person I see?
Will I bring it home?
Will I get it?
What if I do?
These questions feel heavy on my heart
as I enter the room
and try to gently speak
over loudly humming machines
to a dying man.
His brown eyes are open
but his gaze is downward;
I try to meet it,
but we never lock.

I share that I can't imagine what he is going through
and wonder how he is feeling,
but he does not respond to me.
I ask if I can hold his hand
and gently reach out.
He grasps it.
I hold it.
I silently pray that he feels love, peace, and safety.
I wonder what these hands have touched,
what his eyes have seen,
who he loved,
what makes him laugh,
his biggest fear,
what he needs in this moment.
His eyes start to close
and his face softens.
I stay there

and my heart sinks when I tell him
it's time for me to go.
I slowly slide my hand out and say,
"I'll hold you in my heart."
His eyes are wide open again.
He tries to reach for my hand
and I take it for a few more
moments,
before releasing.

I carefully peel off the gear,
scrub my hands,
lean against the hallway wall,
close my eyes,
take a deep breath,
and place my hand
on my heart.

— Rev. Laura D. Johnson

Vespers

You slip mint lip balm into the pocket of your scrubs,
as your tube of Cosmic Crush collects dust in the drawer.
Long ago you traded hoops for studs the shape of stars
that don't snag on the loops of your mask. At night

your resiliency seems to have slipped
off a hook like the bathrobe you trip over
filling your empty coffee mug with water,
cool from the tap. You are starting to feel

the edges of you dissolve. People say
things are not going to be like this forever but
you have seen how it can go from worse to worse.
Today a patient tells you she likes the stars

of your earrings, says she saw a sky so dark once,
it was like salt spilled on a black table cloth. You couldn't see
your hand in front of your face, all you could do was stay
still and let night live all around you.

— Rev. Molly Bolton

Bedside Prayers

For ICU nurses

Loving and gracious God, thank you for this nurse who is giving it their all to restore health and life to the patients they are charged with. Thank you for giving them the courage to come in every shift. May you continue giving them courage, especially when they are fearful. May you guide this nurse with your wisdom, compassion, and love. May they be able to feel your comforting presence surrounding them in their highest of highs, their lowest of lows, and every space in between. Guide these hands as they work to bring healing to each patient. Fill their heart with hope as they see the ways in which you are working in them and through them.

For chaplains

Loving and gracious God, you have called us to be vessels of your healing and love in this world. Help us to be guided by your wisdom, grace, and mercy as we share in the suffering of those around us. Help us to be fully present with every patient, every staff member, and every family that has asked us for help. Allow us to feel your presence with us every single moment of every single day. Quiet all voices but your own so that the words we speak are from you alone. When we are feeling unsure, give us courage; when we are feeling lost, lead us; when we are feeling overwhelmed, bring us peace. We ask for all of these things as your humble and faithful servants.

Prayer for staff at time of patient death

Loving and gracious God, we thank you for this life. We thank you for the hands that worked so hard to save them. We thank you for the ways in which your child has impacted this world. We pray for the family and friends that they leave behind, asking that your comforting presence be felt by them in the depths of their despair. We pray for peace and understanding during this time of loss, and we especially pray for all those who worked to bring healing to this person.

We lift up all of these prayers in your holy name. Amen.

— *Leslie Deslauriers*

Blessing of Nursing and Caregiving Hands

The following is adapted from the 2020 Nurses Week Hand Blessing Ritual at Rush University Medical Center.

Thank you for receiving this time of blessing. We intentionally pause to celebrate you, to celebrate nurses and care-givers—your kindness, your courage, and your impact. As much of the world practices distancing, the closeness of your hands to the lives of your patients is so valuable.

Holding hands is an intimate gesture, one we might do with close friends, family, or our partners. It reflects closeness and trust, connection and relationship. The work you do as nurses and caregivers is often vastly more personal and reflective of this intimacy. Your hands make all the difference in the lives of those in your care. Your hands can turn a moment of fear or anxiety into a moment of compassion and trust.

Look at your hands. Depending on whom you ask, there are 29 bones there, 123 named ligaments, and 48 named nerves. They all work together so that your hands can answer a phone call from a patient's family member as well as securely tie a gown around your waist. Your hands reposition patients into greater comfort and administer medication. Your hands type countless chart notes and rub together under water and sanitizer what feels like an infinite number of times. They do the work that is the most necessary, the most difficult—as well as that which is most sacred.

Prayer

Holy God, Spirit of Love, we thank you for these hands—for the warmth they convey and the strength they possess. Wherever we go, make them instruments of the peace that surpasses understanding. Guide these hands toward justice, in service, with joy. Amen.

— Rev. Ally Vertigan and Rev. Mishca R. Russell-Smith

COVID Collects

Early on in our pandemic-related shutdowns, I found myself praying early and often for frontline healthcare workers and for those most at risk because of health, status, or resources. About a month into working from home, I felt moved to start writing prayers for some of the other folks for whom I was grateful during the early months of the pandemic, which then led into the writing of a series of collects. A collect is a traditional prayer type, consisting of a particular structure of address, acknowledgement, petition, aspiration, and conclusion, whose name likely derives from the sense in which this prayer "collects" the individual prayers of a congregation into one. All of these scribbled COVID collects were heartfelt, some were punny, and each of them expressed prayerful care for the common good in the midst of an intensely challenging time.

Gathering these collects together in the context of this book of prayers, I find myself reflecting on healthcare workers both as people in need of "praying for," and also people who, like so many of us, are searching for the words to pray for others. Doctors and nurses are also parents and children, neighbors and friends, and people of faith who reach for language of care, compassion, and intercession. They are worshippers who miss gathering and singing together, the crumbling bread of shared communion, and the hugs and handshakes of passed peace. What's more, healthcare contexts are themselves communities filled with people of all professions, not only as patients, but also employees who maintain the complex ecosystem of a hospital or treatment facility. The essential workers of the frontline healthcare context treat patients, yes; but they also clean surfaces, remove the garbage, keep the cafeteria running, make sure children being treated are staying caught up on school, and so much more.

Here, then, is a collection of collects, a gathering of gathering-up prayers, that seek to give language of care in the midst of persistent crisis. Collect prayers emerge from the Christian language of prayer and traditionally end with Trinitarian language, often "through Jesus Christ, who reigns with you and the Holy Spirit, one God, now and forever." Since these prayers are intended for an ecumenical and interfaith audience, we have provided alternative concluding language; those praying are, of course, free to use the more traditional ending as they see fit. My hope is that these prayers give words to prayers both for and by healthcare workers, and all those whose work makes theirs possible.

A collect for those most at risk for COVID-19:

God of Refuge,

You protect the weak, comfort the afflicted, and ensure justice for the oppressed. Breathe your life-giving Spirit into those most at risk in a perilous time, that their breath and bodies may know the healing power of your love, all in the name of the One who may always be found with the most vulnerable. Amen.

A collect for nurses, doctors, and healthcare workers:

God of Healing and Hope,

We are made in your image, and our true restoration is found in you. Guide, encourage, and protect all those who are providing critical care during this pandemic crisis, that your love may show forth in health and wholeness for all; all in the name of the Great Physician. Amen.

A collect for researchers, epidemiologists, and vaccine developers:

God of Insight and Inspiration,

You are the source of all truth. Grant your vision and understanding to all those who are researching this virus and developing vaccines and therapies, that their efforts may bear fruitful discoveries for the good of all. Amen.

A collect for healthcare chaplains and others providing spiritual care:

O God Who Covers Us,

You encircle us with your compassion. Grant your heart to all chaplains and those who provide spiritual care, that they may know that heavy burdens are lightened by your love and that the challenges of PPE, closed doors, enforced distance, and remote connections may be protective but not prohibitive, boundaries that communicate love rather than barriers to care. Amen.

A collect for postal workers and delivery drivers:

O God of Deliverance,

Throughout the ages you have inspired your earthly messengers
to share good news through letters and gifts. Bless and protect
postal workers and delivery drivers, that we may be reminded
of our connection across the miles; through the great Bearer of
Good News. Amen.

A collect for stock clerks and grocery store employees:

God of Abundant Provision,

You ensured your people would have enough food to eat even in
the middle of the wilderness. Protect and encourage stock clerks
and grocery store employees, and guide us to truly value their
work, that we may receive the gift of daily bread. Amen.

A collect for cleaning staff and environmental services personnel:

O God who cleanses our hearts,

You healed Naaman through washing in the river, reminding your people of the small miracles which give us life. Protect and sustain cleaning staff and environmental services personnel, whose work is so vital in preventing the spread of viruses and infection. Amen.

A collect for midwives, doulas, and OB-GYNs:

God of Life,

In your love we are born anew. Protect and sustain midwives, doulas, and OB-GYNs as they accompany new and expectant parents during an anxious and scary time, and teach us all to be midwives of the New Creation; in the name of the One born to give us second birth by the power of the Holy Spirit, one God, now and forever. Amen.

A collect for sanitation workers and waste management professionals:

God of All Creation,

In your divine economy nothing is wasted, and we long for all things to be gathered up in you. Protect and sustain sanitation workers and waste management professionals, that we may all be stewards of your creation. Amen.

A collect for scholarship, for all who continue to learn—remotely or in person—with inspiration from Philippians 1:9:

God of All Wisdom,

You have gifted us with learning and scholarship that we might seek growth, truth, and understanding. Sustain and inspire all who continue to learn together in this time, students and teachers, parents and children, that "our love may overflow more and more with knowledge and full insight." Amen.

A collect for farmers, agricultural workers, and food processing workers:

God of the Harvest,

By your grace Jesus fed the hungry and shared stories of your kingdom of shared abundance in the language of seeding and planting, harvesting and threshing. Sustain and protect farmers, agricultural workers, and food processing workers, that we may all cultivate abundant life for each other. Amen.

A collect for the U.S. Capitol switchboard operators who have been hearing my voice—a lot:

Still-Speaking God,

You have sent your Spirit to be our Advocate, and you call us to speak truth to power. Sustain and encourage the U.S. Capitol switchboard operators, that the call to a new creation may be answered even in the halls of Congress. By your Spirit. Amen.

A collect for those for whom grocery store runs were already a source of anxiety:

God of Peace,

You spoke to your servant Abraham in a deep and terrible darkness. Make your accompanying presence known to those for whom the contours of anxiety, fear, and discouragement are all too familiar, that all may walk in your way and know a future with hope. Amen.

A collect for furry, scaled, and winged companions, and the veterinary workers who care for them, with thanks to Cecil F. Alexander and Jurgen Moltmann:

God of All Things,

You made all creatures great, small, and in-between. Bless and keep our furry, scaled, and winged companions, and the veterinary workers who care for them, that we may know ourselves as created and loved both *imago dei* and *imago mundi*. Amen.

A collect for artists of all kinds, with thanks to Gungor:

Creator God, Creative God,

You make beautiful things out of dust. Breathe your inspiration into artists of all kinds, that their works may be a means of grace for us all, deepening our encounter with your creation and provoking us to joy; in the name of the One who gives life, one God, now and forever. Amen.

A collect for folks trying to figure out how to launch books or other new projects right now, with a nod to Jane Parker Huber:

Creator God, Creating Still,

You promise that you are doing a new thing. Encourage and uplift authors and artists attempting to launch new projects in the midst of a pandemic, that through them we may receive a fresh word of inspiration. Amen.

A collect for all of us saddened by the accumulating data about singing and the coronavirus, with thanks to Psalm 126:

God of Songs and Silences,

You have promised that those who sow in tears will reap with shouts of joy. Encourage and sustain us, your singing people, that we all may hear the true, life-giving song of your new creation. Amen.

A blessing for putting on a face mask:

O Lord, Great Giver of Life,

You remind us that to love you, we must love our neighbors. Bless this simple, loving action, that life may be preserved and your love shown forth. Amen.

A collect for those who pray and are running out of words, with inspiration from Romans 8:26:

Still-Speaking God,

Your voice called creation into being, and when we do not know how to pray, your Holy Spirit cries out within us. Give those who pray in your Name the right words to say and the right silences to keep, that we may experience mutual encouragement during this trying time. Amen.

— *Rev. David Finnegan-Hosey*

Prayer for an EMT

Dear Lord, I thank you for the blessings you give, whether I can
see and know them or not. Thank you for your call to me to
serve as an EMT for the health and wellbeing of your children,
my brothers and sisters. Give me wisdom that comes from your
wisdom. Guide my hands, my mind, my heart, my spirit. Give me
speech that helps. Help me in all that I do to be a channel of your
love, your grace, your goodness, your compassion. Make me an
instrument of your healing and your peace. Please bless and be
with those whom I serve and help, their families and loved ones,
and all who care for and about them. And, finally, be with me
and all EMTs who serve your children. This I pray in Your Holy
Name and for the same of all Your children.

— *The Most Rev. Michael B. Curry*

Seen All Along: A Sestina for the Helpers

What if you'd known that this would last so long,
seen into the future, before it began, seen the world
   wearing masks,
seen signs with strange, stern orders to "Stay Six Feet Apart"
   and "Maintain Physical Distance,"
seen your dearest ones' faces behind the gleam of blue-light
   screens?
Where would you have run? Whose body would you have
   rushed to touch?
How would knowing, somehow beforehand, have changed the
   way you've borne this weight?

But you didn't know—no one did—that this wait
(for flattened curves, for vaccines, for glimmers of hope)
   would be so long.
You didn't know the echoing loneliness, the absence of
   human touch,
or how you'd miss seeing sly smiles and flirty pursed lips now
   hidden behind masks,
that you'd find hours of companionship and consolation from
   a computer screen,
or that, in odd and meticulous ways, your heart would begin
   to recalibrate time and distance.

Day by day, month by month, and by sheer will you've gone
the distance,
carried the bulky and awkward weight
of sorrow and sanitizing, of sanity and standing for hours
behind screens,
wondering if offering a message of hope might help
someone along,
if kind words might bring comfort, despite being muted
behind your mask.
Sometimes all you can do is reach out a gloved hand in
silence, lending a latex touch.

In the early months, the helpers were celebrated, and you
were touched
by the attention, by the pot-banging and seven o'clock cheers
from a distance,
but now, your face creased and bruised by the tight grip of
your mask,
no words, no clapping, no free pizza or cup of coffee lifts
the weight
of your spirit. The days are just so very long.
You wish you could stay home, lock the door, and hide, just
gazing into a TV screen.

But please know: You are not invisible behind the glass and
   plastic and plexiglass screens.
We *see* you. We *see* your resolve and the power of your touch.
With you, we all long
to close the distance,
to end the waiting,
to breathe fresh air deeply, freed from our masks.

Imagine looking into a crystal ball with me: See the future,
   unmasked.
Watch yourself exiting the program, making a pixelated screen
go black, when, at last, the wait
is over. Imagine the joy of thrilling, skin to skin touch.
Imagine a hand in yours, ungloved, fingers interwoven,
   no distance
between, when, finally, we can say we have made it through
   this time, after so long.

Today, may you feel the presence of the unmasked One,
   enveloping you in loving touch,
a love not arbitrated by a screen—never remote, never distanced.
May you trust that the Divine One knows the weight you hold
   and sees how strong you've been,
all along.

— *Jennifer Grant*

For the One I Cannot Visit

For the gift of life you have given this your beloved child, we
thank you.
For the love with which he is surrounded when we cannot be
together, we thank you.
Strengthen and bless those who are caring for him when
we cannot.
Bless their families at home.
Bless all of our worry, every fear that enters our hearts,
and mold it into trust in you, whatever happens.
When life ends, put all of us in mind of the love that never ends,
in the life that encircles and contains this world we love.
We entrust our beloved to you in an embrace that is yesterday,
today, and tomorrow.
Amen.

— *Rev. Barbara Cawthorne Crafton*

Remembrance Gathering: A Way to Honor and Release Patients Who Have Died

Note: The practice below acknowledges a group gathering; however, you may choose to read, remember, and honor on your own at any time.

We begin a Remembrance Gathering by passing around a small bowl of smooth, richly colored glass beads shaped like small river stones. (You are welcome to adapt this using any other objects you would like: actual stones, flowers, pieces of paper with names or initials written on them, etc.) We say the names of persons we remember and offer memories to acknowledge their humanity and our shared loss. We then place each glass bead (or other object) in a large Remembrance Vase, and continue with the invitations below.

Before we return to the work of our lives,

let us close this time of remembrance with four brief pauses

to mark these lives, and this time together, as sacred, special—

set apart from our daily routines,

maybe even holy.

First, we pause to honor the fullness of these patients:
Their lives, their loves, their losses, and their legacies.
Hold these people gently in your mind.
Send out the light of comfort to their loved ones.

*Hold a few moments of silence, breathing in love and breathing
out comfort.*

Next, we pause in thanksgiving:
For each of these patients who trusted us with their care.
For each of you, treating every patient with dignity
and respect.
Fill this next quiet with gratitude
for these lives we have named
and for the chance to work as healers, comforters, and
companions.

*Hold a few moments of silence, breathing in compassion and
breathing out gratitude.*

Now we pause to let go,
releasing ourselves from their care,
releasing their suffering,
and releasing our fears for them.

Hold a few moments of silence, breathing in trust and breathing out peace.

Finally, we invite in renewed compassion,
preparing ourselves to continue caring,
continue loving, continue learning.

Hold a few moments of silence, breathing in kindness and breathing out love.

Thank you
for being here to honor these lives.
And thank you
for the care you pour out among us,
every day.

Amen, Ameen, Ashe *(optional)*

— *Rev. Katherine K. Henderson*

A Meditation for Releasing Those Who Have Died

Because we care for people who suffer from many different life-threatening illnesses, we experience a good deal of loss. We may sometimes feel helpless to make any "real" difference in someone's outcome, and sometimes we may feel we are inadvertently contributing to suffering. It is important for each of us to find practices that help us process our sorrow and any other painful feelings that may arise in this work so we can be available to our families and to the next person to whom we offer our professional skills and compassionate hearts.

This meditation might be used as a way to offer loving-kindness to those who have died—as a way of letting them go, or whenever thoughts of someone you knew and cared for arise in your mind. You are welcome to alter these words to best fit your beliefs, values, or desire to bless.

May life lovingly embrace you

May your memory be a blessing

May your loved ones be well and happy

May your soul be satisfied

After you have done this for particular people you remember, you may want to offer this to those who have died whom you did not personally know, mindful of our common mortality.

> *May life lovingly embrace each of you*
> *May your memories be a blessing*
> *May your loved ones be well and happy*
> *May your souls be satisfied*

When you are done, simply allow yourself to rest quietly for a moment in the space of loving-kindness and remembrance without regret.

— *Rev. Ellen M. Swinford*

Blessing for the End of This Year

This year too, butterflies flew thousands of miles,
Hummingbirds ate enough,
People were saved.
This year too, men planted roses,
Women wrote novels,
People left relationships that made them doubt themselves.
This year too, parents spooned applesauce into infants' mouths,
And adults fed their parents in beds with old quilts.
This year too was marked by
What has always held the world—
Tenderness,
Sacrifice,
The luminous,
And you, still in it.

— Rev. Laura Martin

For Your Heart

The root of courage
is a Latin word
meaning "heart."

So
to take "Courage, dear heart"
is to hold up a mirror
and look.

And see . . .

— Rev. Mandy Mizelle

A Prayer in Times of Grief

This is a prayer for when grief doesn't have words.
Or there are too many for the throat to release at once.
When grief has tears. But also a vastness of empty space that
looks like looking off into the distance
or unable to keep commitments.
When time and space stand still and fly by all at once,
and you look up to see that you are still here, even though
grief felt like it might swallow you—
a burning bush yourself. Cloaked many days, yet not
consumed and the divine calling you by name, simply to
announce you are not alone even in this wilderness.

This a prayer that requires no words.
Presence only.
That asks for nothing but offers space to breathe and be,
say *I am still me.*
But I miss people. practices. places. I once knew.
To be held by the ancestors who know pain that requires
a pause even if they couldn't take it.
To be caressed as you rest by those beings who have
always offered unconditional love to lift you along the way.
To hear the voices of those you loved who have left,
whispering . . . *I am here.*

And
you can still miss me.
To remind yourself there's no "should" in grief.
No excellent way to do it.

This is a prayer because the divine doesn't require formalities
to know the heart's petitions.
A prayer when grief doesn't have words.
Or there are too many for the throat to release at once.
So we sit. We stare. We pause. We know. We are.
Grateful that it is all prayer.

— Rev. Chelsea Brooke Yarborough

Ora Pro Nobis

A man lies face down
on the sidewalk
weeping.

In our neighborhood,
the parish church built a candlelit shrine
at street level.

The church is closed for public safety,
but people need to pray,
"to earnestly implore," the dictionary says.

Only those facing darkness can dig deep enough to do this
—humiliation, submission, strength—
to lie on the ground,
to speak the unmentionable out loud
        and demand to be heard,
to bare your soul
        and ask something in return.

Have you ever stepped, solitary, into the void
and felt the weight of it

and the silence?
Rather than papering over it with Netflix or
shouting into Twitter,
 just naked and still in the eye of the storm?

Prayer, they say,
is pounding a vending machine,
writing to Santa,
or worse, commanding a servant:
 do my bidding or else.

But to me,
prayer is stepping into the ring to stare down an ancient opponent
 Despair
  Suffering
   Fear
and staying there, though I cannot win,
 wrestling, wrestling,
and staying there, though I am nearly defeated,
pleading with God to show up and
waiting
 waiting
  waiting

like a man lying face down
on the sidewalk
weeping.

          — *Catherine McNiel*

A Prayer for Naming When It Hurts

God—

We hurt.
Every fiber of our being hurts at times, if not all times.
There's only so much death, pain, and isolation any one of
us can take.
Too often the pain moves us to numbness and platitudes
because we believe that's all we can handle as we're simply
trying to survive.

But Liberating One, create for us and with us spaces that
move past platitudes and "How are you?"
Give us courage to move toward the raw, honest depths to ask
ourselves and one another instead, "Where does it hurt?"

Help us understand it is in naming what's really happening
below the surface that our numbness can begin to subside and
feelings re-emerge.
Remind us that you are a safe space to name our hurts.
Gently nudge us to lay bare and offer up for healing
transformation all our grief and pain.
Comfort us as we move from survival to cleansing breath.

"Where does it hurt?"

It's a vulnerable, bold question, God, for both the one who asks and one who answers.

Give us strength to ask and answer.

Buoy us with hope for what may become when we do.

. . . Grace-filled Tears.

. . . Liberating Release.

. . . Centering Joy.

. . . Rooted Living.

Amen

— *Rev. Molly Brummett Wudel*

Lament

Short on masks.
Short on staff.
Short on rent.

In line for groceries.
In line for nasal swabs.
In line for a shot in the arm.

Short on ventilators.
Short on rooms in my apartment.
Short on hours in the day.

Unprecedented times that didn't have to go like this.
Historic times that maybe didn't have to happen at all.
Exceptional times that exceptional people get to avoid
all together in their vacation homes.

Short on coping skills.
Short temper with my kids.
Short hair I cut off myself.

I don't want to be a hero, I want to sleep at night.

I don't want to be a hero, I want to hug my mom.

I am not a hero, I am . . .

Short of breath.

Shortchanged on my check.

Short on spaces in the morgue.

Beds full of patients.

Streets full of protesters.

Jails full of people,

but soon they'll be empty.

Dying is not the only way

we can be set free.

— *Rev. Molly Bolton*

Blessing for Anger

When the pandemic came
>   your healthcare institutions were unprepared to protect you
>   your government failed to provide what was needed
>   your neighbors ignored the warnings

We saw your interviews on the evening news
>   we heard your pleas
>   we saw your tears
>   we moved on

Anger was the only tone you had left
>   it energized you
>   it uttered powerlessness
>   it protected you from grief

What else could you do
>   you cared for the sick
>   you watched over the dying
>   you placed yourself in constant danger

And we held you on a hero's pedestal while the world burned

Your anger is holy insight into a just world waiting beyond
this moment

> you've watched healthcare inequity kill the poor and
> marginalized
> you've seen apathy allow the elderly to die before their time
> you've known the true toll of this moment far clearer than
> those of us on the outside

Divine anger breaks injustice and re-creates a just world

> anger rejected fasts and sacrifices while the poor starved
> anger turned over money changers' tables that defrauded
> the poor
> anger casts down the mighty from their thrones and lifts
> up the humble and meek

Blessed are the angry

> for their hearts will be open to deeper compassion
> for they have known the true pain of grief
> for they have touched the fiery presence of the divine

May you honor and bless your anger

> let it kindle the divine love of justice in your soul
> let it enlighten your vision to see what a just world could be
> let it energize you to champion justice and end health
> inequity

Amen

— Rev. James Adams

Prayer for Grief's Lessons

God of the sorrowful heart

We pray for all who never asked to be students of grief

We pray for the sudden, the tragic, the slow, and the natural deaths

We pray for the cries, for the sighs, for the moans, and for the
shouts of goodbye

We pray for the empty, cold, lonely, and hard places where
grief hides

We pray for a softening of the lessons of grief

We pray for a smoothing of the rough edges of broken hearts

We pray for a comforting of the wounded and lost self without
the other

God of mercy, we pray that you wipe away the tears of grief

God of grace, we pray that you hold us while we are still hurting

God of love, we pray for spiritual connections to the departed

May our grief teach us new ways to love all whom we have lost

Amen

— *Rev. Dr. Sarah Griffith Lund*

Wilderness (How Hagar Felt)

A Prayer

God of our weary years, God of our silent tears.
This must have been how Hagar felt.
Alone, isolated in this wilderness.
I find myself like her: alone, isolated in this hospital bed.
This must have been how Hagar felt.

Pregnant, with new life in the womb, yet trapped in the
prison of this wilderness. I find myself like her, pregnant with
new hopes and dreams, yet trapped in the prison of this
pandemic. This must have been how Hagar felt.

Bruised and bloody, beaten and bewildered from the physical
hands of Sarah and the lack of boundaries from Abraham.
I find myself bruised, beaten, and bewildered from the
hands of capitalism and the limited respirators from the
government. I can't breathe.
This must have been how Hagar felt.

Now a voice beckons for me to go back home. Back to more
abuse? Back to more judgmentalness and envy? Why should I
leave this wilderness to return to another? I find myself longing

to go back, back to the days before COVID-19, but what am I
longing to return to? Pre-COVID, I found myself in these other
wildernesses of poverty and unemployment?
Why should I leave this wilderness to return to another?
This must have been how Hagar felt.

God, deliver an answer.
Hear the cries of your most vulnerable.
Don't allow injustice to have the final say.
Free us from the torment of our minds.
Allow our future "Ishmaels" to have a place at the table
after this pandemic wilderness ceases.
Give us hope. Give us peace.
This must have been how Hagar felt.

Amén.

— *Rev. Dr. Danielle J. Buhuro*

Intercessory Prayer for Pandemic Frontline Workers

Prayers of intercession are brave prayers. They speak our needs directly to God. They are not shy prayers or pretty prayers. Prayers of intercession give us a space to get gritty and real with the God that walks with us through all parts of our lives, both profound and mundane.

> *"For God has not given us a spirit of fear, but of power and of love and of a sound mind."*
>
> — 2 Timothy 1:7 (NKJV)

God of Wilderness Wanderings, you have seen our confusion. You have seen us pivot to new protocols and new knowledge every month, week, and day of this year. We know more than we did, but God, we are still wandering in a wilderness of pandemics. Give us the fortitude to keep going, the flexibility to keep turning ourselves toward knowledge and love.

We lift up our hearts.

God of the Lost and the Found, we have lost our way and found our way back to you every hour of every day. We are grateful for your steady presence when we are at our least stable. Give us this day, and all the days going forward, signs of hope, of being found by you and by each other. Surprise us with your presence, delight with us in being found again and again.

We lift up our hearts.

God of Blessings of Baptisms, how many times have we come home from our work and stripped and showered before we touched the faces of our beloveds? How many layers of sanitizers have been applied to our chapped and dry flesh? How many more soap and hot water baptisms must we partake in before we are soaked in the cool, healing water we long for? God, you have made us a part of your holy family just by creating us. Help us find ways to renew ourselves that do not sting or chap or separate us from you.

We lift up our hearts.

God of Compassion, we are exhausted. Our hearts keep pulling blood through veins and arteries, but we are tired. Forgive us for unkind thoughts about those we care for. Let us forgive ourselves those thoughts and feelings that come to us when we are aching and unheard. Free us for the wry laughter of the gallows, knowing that your healing comes from strange sources. Give us hearts that are tender enough to care and tough enough to serve.

We lift up our hearts.

God of Rest, even Jesus was overwhelmed by his work and took a nap in a boat. Give us a safe place to rest; give us a clear mind to allow us to rest. God, give us time and a decent mattress and a place to put on clean pajamas and let us rest. Let us wake without dread one day, so that we may continue to answer our calls.

We lift up our hearts.

God of Mourning, we know that the losses are vast, but they are also particular. Know our individual pain and losses even as we commemorate a year's worth of pandemic death. Know our grief as it truly is: full of guilt, relief, pain, shock, failure, hope, memory, and love. Give us the strength to mourn. Give us compassion for others who mourn. Give us words of love and not platitudes. Give us tears, laughter, memories, and fellow travelers to grieve alongside.

We lift up our hearts.

God of Abundant Hope, it has been hard to find you lately. Even with vaccines being given, and the glimmer of light on the horizon, we are still filled with anxiety. You have not given us a spirit of fear, but of love and of power and of a sound mind. God, help us to find that spirit. Help us to know that we are your perfect creation. Let us feel your delight.

Lift up our hearts.

Hear these prayers, God.

Hear our complaints and our musings. Hear the prayers that are too secret to say aloud, to even whisper. Hear our hopes and our fears. Keep us close; help us to feel your presence. We lift up our messy and broken hearts to you. We lift up our imperfect and honest prayers to you.

We lift up our hearts.

Amen.

— Heather Bachelder

A Lament for Composting Hard Truths

> There's a big difference between "staying positive" and being generative. The first disregards hard truths, the second is the fruit of having composted them.
>
> —Toko-pa Turner

We, the Hospital—
We exist for hard times
We are the seasoned nurse and doc and chaplain who have walked through hard truths and handled the heavy
We are the EVS worker who cleans up post code and the dietary worker bringing the comfort cart to the bereaved
And we are all the helpers of the "First-Time-It-Happened-To-Me" workers
    normalizing, stabilizing,
    coming back to work the next day
        . . . or not

Enter COVID-19 stage right

Seeping into our lives, our work, our hospitals,
        our homes, our schools, our houses of worship,
        our gyms, our outdoors, our relationships

So we buckle down and buckle up
We shore ourselves up for the long haul
And the long haul hauls on

COVID-19 seeps into the corners of our hallways,
          into our fears, our identities,
          our questions, our vulnerabilities
          in our hearts and souls and minds

And we haven't shored up enough
          we haven't stored for the hurricane
          we haven't stocked for the famine
          we haven't hoarded enough to sustain
                    body-mind-spirit

The long haul is too long
          out of gas, out of positivity,
          out of energy, out of fire,
          out of nourishment,
          out of wellness resilience coping strategies
                    even with scores of webinars, Zoom
                    meetings, and online support groups

And still COVID-19 seeps
          into our futures, our hopes, our dreams,
          our corners, our blind spots, our weary weariness

Our distractions distract no longer
Our routines stifle us
Our smiles annoy us even under the masks we try not to hide
from ourselves

>Is this sustainable?

>Are WE sustainable?

Eventually, may we have some fruits from composting these hard
truths and realities in which we live;
>may it be generative fruit that is sweet and healthy for us

But right now, it's bitter and dry and unsatisfying and unsustaining

And you bet we're composting—
>racing thoughts have exercised into dysmorphia
>>pummeled prayers have made the voice hoarse
>>>the spirit slumped from perpetuity

The therapy and creativity
>and trying this and trying that
>and trying to be mindful, mindful, mindful
>>until the mind is too full
>>the heart rigid
>>the spirit demoralized

And still COVID-19 seeps and merges
        seeps into apathy and merges until all apathies are
        diseased by apathies

Self-quarantine our apathies in our prisons created for it
        "You should embrace the reality," the therapies say,
        but the apathies are too dangerous to be out in public
            or private
                the apathies seep into words and thoughts
                and mind and spirit

The virus of our apathies is more dangerous than any COVID-19
        or Ebola or Bubonic Plague
        or colonization, or genocide
        or systematic racism
            or Twitter storm

The guardians of our apathies are doing double shifts
        undressing in garages and laundry rooms
            and showering and showering
            and washing hands and washing hands
            and sanitizing and sanitizing
            and singing happy birthday so many times that we
            many need to create a new happy birthday song
            someday to not be traumatized by the song . . .

Will systematic racism end with a vaccine?

Will timid Hope yet spring eternal?

Or must we endure more Winter?

— *Rev. Kelly Gregory*

A COVID-19 Compline

Adapted from The Book of Common Prayer *for 2020–21*

Keep watch, dear Lord, with those who work—
who gather suffering into their arms, who courageously enter the
house of death protected only by a layer of cotton.

—and watch—
as their beloved ones disappear through hospital doors, then are
sent home to wait, alone, in quarantine.

—and weep—
for they cannot be present to sit vigil through the longest night,
to hold that precious hand one last time. Who must learn to say
goodbye through a screen.

Give rest to the weary, bless the dying, soothe the suffering, pity
the afflicted, shield the joyous; and all for your love's sake. Amen.

Lord, in your mercy, hear our prayer.

— Catherine McNiel

Embracing Humankind

Dear G-d,

Sometimes I feel that we, the human race, are battling each other, competing against one another from so early an age.

Children are tested before kindergarten
to determine if they merit entering a gifted and talented program.

Young students compete against each other for grades, spots on sports teams, and in the arts.

Sadly, we have not learned how to wholeheartedly work with each other toward common goals.

COVID is a terrifying and humbling teacher,
showing that what is most essential is not racing against one another,
but, rather, racing toward one another,
to exemplify our other name, *humankind*:
to be gentle, to support each other, and keep one other safe.

We, Your children, beautifully diverse inside and out,
are even more connected to each other than we realized
prior to COVID.

As You, the Ultimate Frontline Worker, support us,
we, Your junior partners, do our best to serve those in our
communities.

As You frequently feel our appreciation, we often feel the gratitude
of our communities.

As You sometimes feel ignored by Your creations, we too
periodically feel overlooked.

As we surpass the unfathomable number of 2.5 million deaths
worldwide,
and 500,000 American lives in just one year,
more deaths than were lost in all the wars our country has fought,
may we realize that each of us is an Essential Worker,
responsible for ourselves and for one another.

As we do our best to embody being *humankind*,
may You graciously continue replenishing us,
enabling us to move forward on our sacred journey
of caring for ourselves and each other.

Amen.

— *Rabbi Deborah Jill Schloss*

I Pray

With holy reverence,

I pray for peace among us as individuals and as a community.

I pray for deliverance for all those in the world afflicted with hate and evil.

I pray for healing where there is brokenness, particularly of the heart and of the spirit, yet also of the mind.

I pray for release from the fear of physical illness and bodily demise.

I pray that songs and words of praise will fill our mouths continually.

I pray for awakening in areas where we are asleep due to ignorance or privilege.

I pray for forgiveness when I have been betrayed or wronged or when I have wronged another.

I pray for comfort when it hurts deep down inside.

I pray for strength in the Divine when we are weak.

I pray for courage to keep trying when it gets hard, to persevere through the pain and challenge.

I pray for joy and laughter that regularly tickle your souls, the kind that sneaks
up on you when you least expect it.
I pray for patience, for we MUST learn to wait on the Holy.
I pray for wisdom in our choices, our actions, and reactions.
I pray for constant guidance and protection from Spirit.
I pray that love prevails—love for God, love for neighbor, love for other, and love
for self.

AMEN

— Rev. Ineda Pearl Adesanya

Prayer for the Dead

("Beloved" can be replaced with the name of the deceased.)

Dear one, as we hold you in our hearts, we see you lifted up in a most glorious, radiant, and holy light. In this pure light, we see you free from the constraints of the flesh with all its frailties and imperfections, its illnesses and pains, its heartbreaks and troubles.

Beloved, we see you lifted up in a light of pure, unconditional love. In this light, you have found the completion of your faith and the perfection of your love. We feel your desire, your hope, and your prayer for us that we make love our journey, so that we may find an even greater love when we make it to our eternal home.

Beloved, we see you lifted up in a light of unspeakable joy and full of glory. The fullness of your joy has come, and it overflows, and is now flowing back to us. We feel your desire, your hope, and your prayer for us that we make joy our journey, so that we may find an even greater joy when we enter our eternal rest.

Beloved, we see you lifted up in a light of everlasting mercy. While on earth, you may have made mistakes and wounded others, and at times been hurt by others, but you have forgiven as much as you have now found forgiveness. We feel your desire, your hope, and your prayer for us that we make forgiveness our journey, that we may find an even greater forgiveness when we enter that everlasting mercy.

And finally, Beloved, we see you lifted up in the light of perfect peace, a peace that surpasses all understanding as you have reached that restful shore of your final destination. We feel your prayer, your hope, and your desire that we will make peace our journey, that we may find an even greater peace when we cross that river at last into our eternal rest.

Beloved, we honor you. Though our hearts are pained at your departure, we are glad you lived!

Amen.

— *Rev. Randy Lewis*

A Litany for Those Who Have Cared for COVID-19 Patients and Their Families

I remember those who contracted and died from the virus. Their breath was labored and they were alone.
Feel free to say name(s) aloud and/or light a votive in their memory.

I remember the families of those who suffered from the virus. They could not linger or touch or be too close.
Feel free to say name(s) aloud and/or light a votive in their honor.

I remember those who struggled with the virus and got better. They healed. They lived to tell of this tale.
Feel free to say name(s) aloud and/or light a votive in their honor.

I remember colleagues who put themselves and their families at risk to do their jobs. They are committed, courageous.
Feel free to say name(s) aloud and/or light a votive in their honor.

As I remember these faces, names, shifts, and interactions, I remember my own part of this Story. I am still here.
You may want to place your hands over your heart or in a prayer position in honor of your own experience.

Closing blessing:

*May I be strengthened in body, mind, and spirit as I continue
my work.*

*May all whom I love and I be healthy and whole, protected from
the virus and keeping it at bay.*

*May there be grace as I continue to struggle and stumble, giving
my imperfect best and trusting it is enough.*

*May all who are within my care experience wellness, tenderness,
respect, and gentleness.*

*May this virus be contained soon, and may all the hard lessons it
is offering us be accepted humbly, with courage.*

Amen. Shanti. Shalom. And may it be so.

— Rev. Hadley Kifner

Written on Your Heart

You are seen, you are heard, and you are known. The care you have provided and continue to provide is seen and appreciated. The daily sacrifice and commitment to those in need does not go unnoticed. May you feel comforted as you are looked upon with love by the One who loves perfectly.

The cry of your heart is heard. As you have grieved the many losses and pains of this pandemic, know the voice of your heart has been heard. Every tear shed for yourself, or for the family who has lost someone dear, has been captured and bottled up. Its meaning has been heard and discerned by the One who gives grace and hears our cries even when they make no sound.

Your burden is known. As you have carried the mounting weight of this past year, you have been seen, heard, and known. May you begin to shed the constant weight you have carried, not forgetting all that has happened, but moving through to the other side so that you may honor those who have so deeply touched your heart.

— *Rev. Drew Phillips*

Healers Needing Healing

We, healers, are some of the ones in need of the most healing.

How much suffering have we witnessed during this pandemic? What pain have we soaked up on this road to collective liberation as we have answered our callings? This is especially true for those of us from marginalized groups who continue to see our communities ravaged by many layers of racism, along with this deadly virus.

Those, like me, who genuinely seek to usher in compassion are exhausted by the immense suffering. Compassion fatigue and vicarious trauma are brutal and unforgiving, bringing about despair and doubt. I, too, am exhausted, wondering what might need to shift within me to endure both the everyday challenges and the momentous, once-in-a-lifetime moments that seem to happen every week.

I find myself recognizing all the ways in which I block my own receiving of grace and care from myself or others. Not slowing down long enough to discern where the spirit truly is leading me to use my gifts, instead relying on my worldly ego that will have me guard my pain behind my role of being a healer and teacher. Inflicting violence upon myself as I run to put out every fire when I am not trusting of the spirit or others to do their part while I restore myself. Truthfully, I can be quite disdainful of my own pain and humanness, which is the very thing that makes me a potent leader. These days, more of me is in need of healing and care. I pray that we, healers, drop fully into our tender spots to allow ourselves to receive the empathy that we so readily offer others. For it is in the receiving that we become restored.

A meditation for all of us who are healers:

May we receive rest and comfort.
May we be vulnerable enough to experience healing.
May we open to our enoughness.
May we discern where we are being called.
May we trust spirit to lead.

— Hayden Dawes

Metta Meditation: A Practice of Loving-Kindness

Metta is a Buddhist practice of loving-kindness for oneself and others. It always begins with loving thoughts for self (often the person we're hardest on!) and then extends out to others. This practice does not require that you believe anything in particular as a matter of religious faith or cultural value. It is a practice anyone can do regardless of one's deepest convictions. It is simply a way of offering care and softening one's heart.

Take a comfortable position that allows you to remain alert with eyes closed or downcast. Take several slow, gentle breaths, and then begin to repeat silently the following good wishes[1]:

> *May I be safe*
> *May I be strong*
> *May my heart be open*
> *May I know peace*

---

[1] You can change these words as you like. For example, you may find it helpful to say, "May I be free from fear," or "May I be joyful."

After some time, extend this wish to someone close to you ("close" can mean either emotionally important to you or simply nearby physically).

> *May you be safe*
> *May you be strong*
> *May your heart be open*
> *May you know peace*

Gradually expand your circle of loving-kindness to include more people, more living beings.

If there is someone in your life with whom you have been in conflict, try sending loving-kindness to them.

In time, perhaps our circle of loving-kindness will expand to include all beings!

When you are done, simply allow yourself to rest quietly for a moment in the space of loving-kindness, without focusing on any thought that may arise.

— *Rev. Ellen M. Swinford*

Two Blessings for Troubled Times (and Troubled Hearts)

I.

Blessed are those who "still aren't over it yet."
Blessed are those who pray with their tears.
Blessed are those who are doing OK.
Blessed are those who aren't doing OK.
Blessed are those who find a way to laugh,
    even though they aren't doing OK.
Blessed are those who are worried.
Blessed are those who help others.
Blessed are those who are kind to themselves.
Blessed are those who believe that healing is possible.
Blessed are those who feel hopeless.
Blessed are those who hold hope for others.

II.

This is a blessing
for the part of you that grieves in secret
yearning for your childhood home
or the sound of your grandmother shuffling cards,
waking up in half-ashamed dreams
of your first lover,

or the time you knew (but then forgot!) how to fly.
This blessing knows you already:
the ways you pretend,
your many kinds of laughter,
the pulse of your worry.
This blessing knows
that you often crave the stars
or the sweat of a dance party,
and that you feel guilty
because you're already so lucky
but you still ache for more.
This blessing can't take away the yearning
but it can draw a connecting line
between your pain and mine,
between pockets of suffering and dreaming.
In the diagram of our grief
maybe there is a pattern of blessing,
a fractal of grace.

— *Rev. Katherine K. Henderson*

For Your Breath

In the beginning,
there was breath,

hovering and humming
over
primordial waters,

uttering in darkness,

blowing into dust . . .

Listen,

you are a conch.

— Rev. Mandy Mizelle

My Lord, What a Morning

I met a woman who liked her hospital bed lowered
to the floor so she could see through her window
as much sky as possible. I don't know why

it took until my back hurt from bending to take
a white towel from the linen closet and spread it out
like a picnic blanket on the grey tile floor. I ask

into her good ear what is giving you strength today
she pauses then opens her mouth to sing. Occasionally,
I can touch that part of me that hasn't moved. The pit

of the avocado as I spoon out flesh. The amaryllis bulb
in the blue ceramic pot by the side door. Every
now and then I feel space expand like sky

spreading orange over beige buildings. Like a blanket
catching breeze before it meets grass. Like the refrain
of a gospel song as more voices join in.

How we used to sing together
before to love someone
was to be far apart.

— *Rev. Molly Bolton*

Breath Prayer

I often begin conversations about spirituality by pointing out that spirituality *shares a root* (spirare) *with words like* respiration *and* inspiration—*words about breath. This shared root between* spirit *and* breath *is also found in the Hebrew Bible, where the word* ruach *means both "spirit" and "breath," and similarly in New Testament Greek, in which* pneuma *means "spirit" and "breath."*

Breath, then, is at the root of our spirituality, and paying attention to breath is something which connects us across religious and cultural differences. I penned the following poem over the summer, when the confounding realities of respiratory pandemic and racist violence made me think all over again about the importance of breath:

I spend so much of my time
inviting people to breathe.
Teaching that breath and spirit are the same word, across
languages, across time;
that God breathes the Spirit that is Life,
the very breath of our lungs.

I spend so much of my time
reminding myself to breathe,
that my body can do this,
that my mind can do this:
Breathe.

But now,
we must be careful with our breaths,
not knowing what they might carry.

And now,
another voice gasps out, "I can't breathe."
Another spirit silenced.

And I tell myself,
"Just breathe."
And I worry about what the word means.
And I wonder at this call:

To take the next breath,
so that our breaths may be the Spirit,
the Spirit that makes a world,
a world where everyone can breathe.

— *Rev. David Finnegan-Hosey*

They Say This Time Is Invaluable

When you care for a dying parent
People will often tell you
In so much earnest
This time with *them* is invaluable

you think
They aren't wrong
But
You wonder
would they like to trade places
to know
how that invaluable time gets filled?

Let me tell you
It's
constant frustration
caregiving and dying
Needing only reprieve from one other
And from the reminder
Of what *is*

the forever
Stale moment of being "present"
Looming
Nowhere to run
So, you sit in the inevitable.

Death
Smells horrible—even from a distance
It clings to everything
Your senses know

existing in this atmosphere
is like having a larger than life "houseguest" that won't leave
but graciously insists you carry on

Rude and overbearing,
laying claim to everything
watching as you take your first sip in the morning—
coffee
lands
tasteless,
your eyes hungrily search surroundings for reprieve
but are met with anxious suffering
and Death
sitting on couches
waiting

you move forward
your first task of the morning, every morning for months
and that which will undoubtedly haunt you forever:
The woman who bore you
doesn't look comfortable in skin anymore
Body made stranger
With lumps and broken skin
spirit fighting everything in its way—you, other helpers, death,
life, and then the sequence
over again . . .
no matter the progression, she is encumbered with limitations
But every once in a while, a sweet message escapes from her spirit
Directed at you
tenderly
and in the silence

"we are not alone"
You listen carefully
smile subtly
to communicate
through the discomfort
and now intimate knowledge that three is most certainly
a crowd.

— *Leenah Safi*

It Is OK to Scream

It is OK to scream.

Go outside and scream at the top of your lungs.
Ignore everyone around you who looks.
They know you are screaming for them, too.

Scream, a primal scream, a scream that ends
in an ugly cry.
You know, that cry that comes in waves.
That catches your breath until you almost pass out.
That cry where your nose is running and just won't stop.
That cry that results in dry heaves.

Scream, cry.
God can handle it.
These are unusual times.
Death is a constant companion.
You watch people die—die without family, without friends.
You ease their journey.
While trying to remain safe for you and yours.

It's been a year. No one anticipated a year.
Maybe a month. Maybe two months. Then three.
Then four, then . . . stop counting.
Because it does not make sense.

What does not make sense is people who don't believe,
don't believe COVID is real.
People, selfish people—it's their right not to wear masks.
A simple mask that could save lives.

So, yes, scream.
Cry, an ugly cry.

But know you are loved. You are appreciated.
Know that we thank you, even when no one else does.
You, who put your life on the line so others might live.
So, scream. Yes, cry.
God can handle it.

— *Rev. Gayle Fisher-Stewart*

A Blessing for the Weary

You who feel lost in the darkness:

    may a beam of light shine on your face and your path.

You who journey through death:

    may you encounter a surprise in the valley, a sign of new life.

You who feel sunk into despair:

    may hope come near to you, for true hope is born in
    the depths.

In exhaustion,

    may you find sleep and rest.

In suffering,

    may you receive peace and relief.

In isolation,

    may you feel presence, a steady hand upon your back.

You who have poured out all that you are:

    may life be restored to you.

You who have lost more than you can face:

    may you discover you are never alone.

You who can go no further:

    may you find strength to lay down in the presence of God.

— *Catherine McNiel*

Blessing for the Night

No matter the time, it is late

God, where are You now?

My blinking eyes can no longer see light

Night shadows search me out

Here in the long night I look for You

Are You here in the night?

Are You here in the silence?

Are You here in the shadows of my soul?

Are You here in the deep loneliness?

Teach me to befriend the dark

Teach me to hear the night rhythms of Your heart

Teach me to discover hope in the shadows

Teach me to find the blessing of You

Here with me

At night within me

One with me

Amen

— *Rev. Dr. Sarah Griffith Lund*

A Prayer for Pandemic Times

O God of hope, O God of our hopefulness,
we come to You in this pandemic time of pandemonium
that seems—that, so far, is—unending, with illness abiding
and death abounding.

As we wait for signs of surcease, we remember that Jesus,
at prayer, watched his disciples struggling against the wind,
and then, coming to them upon the water, the gale ceased.

O God, by Your Spirit, free our hearts of fear, unshackle our
souls that we, continually, may lift our hands in supplication
unto You; especially that You, with sustaining strength, will fill
to overflowing the cups of care and confidence of our sisters
and brothers devoted to medical professions, who live and
move and have their being to serve and to save.

All this we ask in Your Name, trusting in the presence and
power of Your Love.

Amen.

— Rev. Paul Roberts Abernathy

Here

Beacons of warning,
Maps webbing terror,
It is coming, it is coming here!

New layers on faces,
Layers scrubbed off hands,
It is coming, it is coming, and soon will be here.

Are you essential? What can you do?
It's coming. Who are you
When it is here?

Halls empty, doors closed
A gallows reprieve? No.
It is coming and soon will be here.

Raw hands, raw eyes, Melpomene faces
Holding and proning.
It is here, it is here.

We breathed their last breaths
Clasped their hands fast. They did not die alone.
There are more, there are more here.

Going slow to go all the way down,
To the quiet places where COVID was,
And COVID took, and God is still here.

— *Rev. Kari Pellegrino*

A Collect for Parents Working on the Front Lines

Loving and gracious God,

Grant that weary parents who work on the front lines might have peace in body, mind, and spirit, that the work they do on behalf of other people's families might not take away from their own.

This we pray with confidence and hope.

Amen.

— *Rev. Traci Smith*

For Those Who Wait

> "[B]ut those who wait for the Lord shall renew their strength,
>   they shall mount up with wings like eagles,
>   they shall run and not be weary,
>   they shall walk and not faint."
>
> —Isaiah 40:31

> "I'll be with you as you do this, day after day after day, right up to the end of the age."
>
> —Matthew 28:20 (MSG)

This is for those of you who know what it means to wait. You spend precious time waiting on and with others. You wait with them as they wade through moments of uncertainty, exhaustion, grief, and the unknown. You understand the ministry of presence through waiting and intentional listening. You understand that waiting is a part of ministry. Life requires moments of waiting, those unexpected and often unwanted pauses that may seem to stop the journey. You comfort others in these multiple moments of waiting.

You know what it means to wait.

You are present in the waiting. In the midst of these waits, you have accompanied others and watched as they have released weights. You accompany them through their journeys.

This prayer is for those of you who know what it means to wait. It is dedicated to the ones who spend time waiting on and with others.

The Creator spends precious time waiting on and with *you*. The Creator is present and with *you* in the waiting as *you* wade through moments of uncertainty, exhaustion, grief, and the unknown. This prayer is a reminder that *you* are accompanied and covered in prayer as *you* wait. May *you* receive moments to refuel in the midst of waits. May *you* be given an opportunity to release some weight while *you* wait.

Remember that *you* are accompanied by the One who understands the ministry of presence and intentional listening. *You* are accompanied by the One who will never leave you and will wait with *you*.

— *Rev. Sheila P. Spencer*

If Words Could Heal

If words alone could heal,
I'd write rivers of Get Betters
and then sleep, knowing
we'd all wake up
the next day.

If my breath created life,
then I wouldn't be afraid
of passing death on,
even as I
pull my mask up.

And if my blood could save,
I'd pack vials of the stuff
and ship it anywhere, everywhere,
first thing and
fast enough.

If my body were a temple
big as Jerusalem,
I'd let everybody in
as could fit
six feet between them.

And if it were bread, well then,
the other horseman, Famine,
would be on his way,
not preying on
our homes.

And if I thought it were enough
to simply pray,
I'd be in church, or Temple,
every single day,
my words, my breath,
my blood and body
something of a hazmat suit
and I'd know that we were
safe.

But since it isn't, can't, and won't,
I'll sing the praises of
those willing souls
so well-versed in
the breath, the body, blood,
doing all they can
to heal, sustain, and
save us.

May these words,
as little as they are,
be blessed enough to
give you
       hope.

— Jessica Covil

A Prayer for a Long Shift

Creator God, you unfurled the world with a Word—
and on the seventh day, you rested.
God, there is no rest for the weary.
We are too tired to observe sabbath,
too wired to sleep.
There is always more to be done,
miles to go before we wake from this nightmare.
Our muscles throb, our heads ache, our hearts break.
Hold us, O Great Physician.
Enfold us in your gentle arms,
returning to us a portion of the care
we share with your people.
Receive our exhausted sighs
as wordless prayers, ever a reminder
that our lungs still rise and fall
with the miracle of breath.
Abiding One, have mercy.
Comforting One, have mercy.
Eternal One, have mercy.
Please.
Amen.

— Rev. Katherine Willis Pershey

InFINITE

G-d, I try to rise to the highest possible version of myself as much as possible, and especially
during more challenging times, like this time of COVID.
But I am afraid that I am not always the best possible arrangement of myself.
Sometimes I feel stuck, robot-like, spent—not a very worthy incarnated associate to You.
And I appreciate that You are not impatient or disappointed in me as I am when I find myself mired in an unflattering configuration.
I draw comfort from knowing You still wholeheartedly embrace me when I am not able to do so myself.
Even though I do not always feel You when I especially yearn for You, I draw sustenance knowing
Your Presence is both within me and envelopes me,
gently and graciously beckoning finite me to revive in Infinite You.
Having felt Your soothing and powerful aura infuse me, Your absence is painfully palpable when I cannot sense Your proximity.

When You hug me and I do not feel it, it is like when a tree falls in an empty forest and no one hears it.

Your hug is as real as the loud sound no one heard.

May Your warm, loving embrace of every aspect of who I am become even more perceptible to me, in turn, allowing me to continue sharing Your energy with others also in need of Your sustenance.

Thank you, G-d, for entrusting me to be one of your many unique earthly partners helping stitch a beautiful and intricate tapestry connecting heaven and earth.

— Rabbi Deborah Jill Schloss

Companioning One

Companioning One,

When the fears rise
and the pressures push
me toward that cursed corner—
the dark and crushing space
saying, "*It all depends on me*"—
help me rise.

Lift me out and above
this swirl of deceptions, God,
and remind me I am not alone,
or expected to know or be or provide
everything.

My eyes just need to be in the right place.

Reground my understanding
that while I am called to faithfulness
with what I have,
where I am,
the make-or-break power of my days
is beyond my skill.

Give me one reminder this week, God,
of your presence in the details—
just enough to shake me from
this stupor of self-reliance.

I commit today's work to you,
and thank you for what you'll
make of it.

Amen.

— Rev. Arianne Braithwaite Lehn

God of It All

God of it all,
Sometimes I prefer the calls that are about healing and birth, joy and going home. The good stuff.
The death, grief, disappointment, and dark can be too much.
Sometimes I'd rather sleep in. I'd rather be outside for starts to new seasons and leaves on the way to crisp color.
Some days I imagine cutting fresh flowers, or baking bread, dancing with children out in the dusty floor of a playground, cleaning a stock room, or filing papers—work that might be easier on the heart, easier on the soul, easier to do and then be done.
Help me limp, crawl, wade, press on through the messed up brokenness that seeks me out.
Give me peace when the pager, the paperwork, the pain of patients and their parents adds up on top of the pandemic and politics and perverse privilege.

And then I remember . . .
I exhale and smile. Release and let go.
All is life. All is service. All is grace. All is joy.
You are God of it all.
You are with me in it all.
You have gone ahead and sent love and it awaits.
And it is well with my soul.

Renew in me a sense of calling and remind me of my love for
wholeness, hope.

Restore in me a humble appreciation for what I have to offer,
what I can offer.

Replenish in me a contentment that is bound in Truth and does
not waver with the news of the world.

Refresh me as only you can, whispering in my ear that rest is
in the Divine, hidden in the Sacred.

And I shall find that rest.

I shall hear Your voice.

I shall offer what I can.

And I shall love, Love, love Love.

With a grateful heart, here I go . . .

Amen.

— Rev. Hadley Kifner

A Prayer at the Conclusion of a Shift

My praises to You, Adonai our God, Spirit of the Universe, I am grateful for Your presence throughout my day. May the work I have done bring a measure of comfort to those in need of healing. I pray that You extend Your compassion to those who reach out to You.

May I continue to draw the breath You breathed into me. May I safely return home to rest and rise again to continue to do Your work.

I thank You for guiding and guarding me throughout this day; may I continue to merit the protection of Your presence.

My praises to You, Adonai, Guardian of Your people and Source of Health.

— *Rabbi Brian T. Nelson*

An Invitation to Breath & Mystery & Courage

Breathe deeply, becoming centered in the here and now, aware of the embrace of this Earth our home, of the life-sustaining air which you, along with all of Earth's breathing creatures, enjoy by continuous exchange with all that is green and growing. May you open your heart and mind to the wonder and mystery that is Life, and with gladness and gratefulness commend yourself and your service to that which draws you to become your best, that in which you place your trust, that which is the source and inspiration of your reverence and your purpose, however it is that you know and name and honor it in the secret places of the heart and in daily practice.

Hold a few moments of silence, rest, reflection, or gratitude.

May these moments reflect and participate in the unfathomable and faithful unfolding of all that makes meaning, engenders integrity, awakens courage, and sustains hope. May you find your daily service endowed with significance beyond your comprehending, that you may experience yourself as collaborator with the Inexpressible in which all things are rooted and through which all things come to fruition in due season.

Hold a few moments of silence, rest, reflection, or gratitude.

May you prepare to take into your hands again the work of this season and the needs of this day, looking forward to harvests of health and wholeness envisioned but not yet attained. May you live and work so as to keep faith always with our common experience of reverence and purpose. In all that you pursue, in all you endeavor to learn and to manage, may you remain, at root, committed to promoting integrity and humility before the great encompassing and commanding Mystery, known by many names and nameless, comprehended by no one, which is as close to you as your own breathing and beyond all you can ever know.

So may it be.

— *Rev. Ellen M. Swinford*

Slow Exhale

Spirit of God, Holy Breath,

my chest is heavy,
my jaw clenched,
my shoulders hunched,
my fingers wrapped tight
around all the things
I am trying to hold.

Breathe in, they say,
roll your shoulders back and down,
breathe into the spaces that feel tense
or painful
or blockaded.

Breathe in.

Sometimes when I say this to others,
I realize what a tell it is,
how soon I say,
"Breathe out,"
and how quick the exhale is,
because the inhale was so shallow.

And so I sit
here
now
prayerful,
trying to open up,
trying to listen for you,
trying to breathe.

Breathe in, I say to myself,
and inhale a little more.

My chest feels tight, still,
my shoulders hunched, still,
but maybe it's a little better than last time.

Breathe in,
and breathe deeper;
feel the inhale to your core.

It's a practice we need now,
because we forget:
the deep inhale
and the pause
to listen

and the
slow
exhale

Amen.

— *Rev. Martha Spong*

For Your Becoming

Bless you,
beloved one,

uniquely and wonderfully made,
worthy to love and be loved
in equal measure.

The world delights
in
and depends
on

your
feet,

hands,

heart,

breath,

b e c o m i n g . . .

— Rev. Mandy Mizelle

Instructions for Anxious Days

Remember what has carried you here,
Through other times when
The earth shook.
Chop vegetables,
Create with your hands,
Stay close to something that
Reminds you of laughter.
Hold a book,
Release a prayer,
Pick up a strand with someone
That you had dropped.
Go into a field
Without any agenda but your presence.
Believe that even now,
The earth is moving toward spring,
And something that has been closed
Will open again,
And the blossom will be
Extravagant.

— Rev. Laura Martin

Litany for Incarnation

Creator God, the story of your incarnation reminds us
that all things come into being through You.

As the year stretches on, we wrestle with the contrasts of being
alive, and we yearn for you to illuminate your place in our lives.

Please, bring us to where you begin:

Bring us to birth—
Let our children ask us questions!
Bring us to death—
Let us tell our stories!
Bring us to plant—
Let us dream of what is to come!
Bring us to harvest—
Let us delight in green blades rising!
Bring us to hurt—
Let us grieve what was good!
Bring us to heal—
Let us repair what was bad!
Bring us to rubble—
Let us defy our defenses!
Bring us to build—
Let us discover our alliances!
Bring us to tears—
Let us wash out our worries!
Bring us to laughter—
Let us shake knots from our bellies!

Bring us to mourning—
>Let us remember!
Bring us to dancing—
>Let us play!
Bring us to scattering—
>Let us trust distance!
Bring us to gathering—
>Let us trust intimacy!
Bring us to embrace—
>Let us feel how our sorrows fit.
Bring us to solitude—
>Let us learn to care for ourselves.
Bring us to scrap—
>Let us save what is special!
Bring us to sew—
>Let us make something new!
Bring us to silence—
>Let us dwell in your Word!
Bring us to speech—
>Let us sing with your praises!
Bring us to love—
>Let us be found!
Bring us to hate—
>Let us get lost!
Bring us to war—
>Let us fight!
Bring us to peace—
>Let us rest.

Amen.

— Claire Repsholdt

Sunrise

As the sun rises in the sky
Over us today and each day
Please wrap your arms around us
And let Your love guide the way
Please give us a sense of peace, hope, love,
And stamina to see this through
Please guide our hands and our minds
In each patient task we do
Please let us also remain aware
Of our co-workers during this time
To ensure that each of us is remaining well
Body, spirit, and mind
Amen

— Jamie R. Rivera

Invocation of Opening the Curtains

God of hope and love—
As we move through our day
Dealing with barriers, distance
Let us see past pandemic blockades, to remember
The sacred that is on both sides

In our familiar homes, beckon us
To open our curtains and blinds
And see what is outside, beyond
Our small view of the world
And help us pause and breathe

The sun is always there, even when cloudy
Breeze that we may not feel, is there too
With birds chirping and plants breathing
It is a much different view of this world
Help us notice such massive and small creations

With all that is on the other side
Of a window, curtain, and blinds
Imagine what is on the other side
Of a mask and six feet of distance
Holding all the complexities of being creation, too

Beckon us to look and listen
Remind us of the sacred that
Is always there
With your love and hope
Sustaining us all.

— Rev. Jessica Stokes

An Invitation

It has been observed by many that human beings order their lives around the easy—and often around the easiest of the easy—but the true challenge is to hold to the difficult. COVID-19 offered an invitation to all of us to hold to the difficult as we were stopped in our busy tracks and challenged to ask a new set of questions.

Once the shock wore off following all of the shutdowns, and the death toll continued to rise, it was no longer possible to believe that this moment would quickly pass by. We could not simply hunker down and wait for it to pass. We had to engage this moment.

But how do you engage such a strange moment? A moment that arrived with so little warning and for which we were so unprepared?

Wise ones among us invited us to *stand still*. We needed to stand still and listen to our hearts. Stand still as one needs to do if lost in the forest and allow the trees to help you find your way out. The trees are not lost. Standing still revealed much to us, including the most important revelation: that COVID-19 is an invitation, indeed. The invitation continues to beckon us toward individual and collective interrogation of ourselves as we imagine the way forward in what is destined, at some point, to become a post-COVID-19 world.

Who do we wish to be and what must we do? How will we order our lives?

— *Dr. Catherine Meeks*

Life Prevails

Death lurks.

> A silent, invisible, threatening pestilence,
> with a smiling face and contagious laugh;
> a killer of dreams, destroyer of purpose,
> holding no respect of persons.
> It offers no Good Friday reprieve;
> observes no blood on the doorpost, no Passover.
> No respect for the aged, the innocent, the believer.
> No regard for the rich, the famous, the politician.
> It steals with impunity and breaks the scales of justice.
> It embraces carelessness, hubris, and the opportunist,
> but carries with it a reckoning, a promise, a forever change.
> Empowered by anguish, indifference, and uncertainty,
> it exacts its fierce toll, exposing our iniquities.
> A collector, ready to claim whomever, whatever, whenever
> it wills—
> it demands audience with all of humanity.

> Will our bodies betray or protect us when it arrives?
> We cannot leave it to chance or blissful ignorance.
> We cover; we distance; we resist, but never surrender.
> Nineteen—a number not of death,
> but of growth and spiritual awakening.

We nod to death's certainty, but not before our time.
With places to go, things to do and see, love to make,
we fight, encourage, strengthen, love and are loved.
Knowing tomorrows were never promised,
we seize the day, living it as it is to be lived,
praying without ceasing, hoping without despair, loving
without fear,
service without suspicion, courage without cruelty,
distance without disconnection.
We awaken from our slumber to redeem our days, to
catch our fall,
to embrace the promise of our standing. If we do
so together,

Life prevails . . .

— Rev. Randy Lewis

Prayer for the Covering

God, cover those we love with your grace
Across the miles where we cannot go
We pray for your Spirit to travel for us
May your Spirit embrace our little ones with delight
May your Spirit hold our dear ones with joy
May your Spirit rock our babies with ancestral pride
May your Spirit cover our hurting ones with love
May your Spirit hold hands with our dying
May your Spirit cover us with hope for tomorrow
Amen

— *Rev. Dr. Sarah Griffith Lund*

God Is Everywhere

A Benediction

Remember that as you go, God is ABOVE you,
watching over you as The Good Shepherd.

God is BELOW you, ready to lift you up into
God's arms in your weakest moment.

God is BEHIND you, giving you encouragement
when you want to give up and turn back.

God is in FRONT of you, calling you forward in faith.

God is BESIDE you, holding your hand no matter
what you are going through.

But most of all, God is WITHIN you,
as close as every breath you take.

And that, my brothers and sisters, makes all the difference.

Amen.

— *Rev. Malcolm L. Marler*

As You Love the Only World We Have

Blessed be your feet,
going into places that others leave,
feeling tired but steady.
May they keep you standing.

Blessed be your hands,
rubbing backs, checking temps and time,
preparing food and medicine.
May they always find palms to hold.

Blessed be your breath,
moving behind the mask,
pumping life to all the limbs.
May it anchor you in this present moment.

Blessed be your eyes,
focusing above the mask, sometimes crying,
saying in the language beyond words—*I see you.*
May they show you more beauty.

Blessed be your mind,
that tackles problems, that imagines solutions,
that gets creative when there are none.
May it dream new dreams.

Blessed be your heart,
that risks its own pain by loving the fearful, the sick, the lonely,
the dying.
May it be brave and not afraid.

Blessed be your body, that cares for another, that moves in closer,
that grieves, laughs, comforts, and prays.
May it know purpose and rest.

May all the gentleness, courage, and compassion
that your one sacred body gives
all flow back to you,
as you love the only world we have.

— Rev. Keith A. Menhinick

Beloved, You Are

Beloved, you were created in light, in story, in song.

Beloved, you radiate, weave, and rejoice.

Beloved, remember that within you is the love that knows no bounds.

Beloved, remember that love as you begin this new day.

Beloved, the power of hope can be found in the sinew of your heart.

Beloved, the hope you feel pulling on your heartstrings is the gift
of our creator, our God.

Beloved, take courage, take heart, and play the song of hope, even
if you are the only one who sways to the melody.

Beloved, this is the creator's favorite tune.

— *Rev. Ginny Wilder*

Contributors

Rev. Paul Roberts Abernathy is a retired Episcopal priest.

Rev. James Adams is a board-certified chaplain specializing in palliative care and bereavement and a priest in the Anglican Church of North America within the jurisdiction of the Armed Forces and Chaplaincy.

Rev. Ineda Pearl Adesanya serves as Associate Minister of Spiritual Life for the Allen Temple Baptist Church and as President/CEO of The *Interfaith* Chaplaincy Institute. She is the editor and coauthor of *Kaleidoscope: Broadening the Palette in the Art of Spiritual Direction.*

Heather Bachelder is a graduate of the Wake Forest School of Divinity and a current student at the Lutheran Theological Southern Seminary. She is a candidate for ordination through the North Carolina Synod of the ELCA.

Rev. Molly Bolton is a chaplain, spiritual director, and writer in Boone, North Carolina.

Rev. Kathy Bozzuti-Jones, PhD, is the Associate Director for Faith Formation and Education at Trinity Church Wall Street in New York City.

Nathan Brown served as Poet Laureate for the State of Oklahoma in 2013–14 and now travels full-time performing readings, concerts, and workshops and speaking on creativity, poetry, and songwriting. Nathan has published over twenty books. Most recent is his new collection of poems now known as the *Pandemic Poems Project*.

Rev. Dr. Danielle J. Buhuro is a CPE Supervisor at Advocate Aurora South Suburban, Trinity, and Christ Hospitals in the Chicago area. She is the author of *Spiritual Care in an Age of #BlackLivesMatter: Examining the Spiritual and Prophetic Needs of African Americans Living in a Violent America*.

Jessica Covil is a PhD candidate in English at Duke University, pursuing graduate certificates in Black studies and feminist studies.

Rev. Barbara Cawthorne Crafton is an Episcopal priest and author.

The Most Rev. Michael B. Curry is Presiding Bishop and Primate of the Episcopal Church. He is the author of *The Power of Love, Following the Way of Jesus, Songs My Grandma Sang*, and *Crazy Christians: A Call to Follow Jesus*.

Hayden Dawes, LCSW, LCAS, is a PhD student at the University of North Carolina–Chapel Hill's School of Social Work, where his research aims to promote the mental health and social well-being of people of color and LGBTQIA+ individuals.

Leslie Deslauriers is a chaplain at Rush University Medical Center in Chicago, Illinois.

Rev. Elizabeth Felicetti is the Rector of St. David's Episcopal Church in Richmond, Virginia.

Rev. David Finnegan-Hosey is the author of *Christ on the Psych Ward* and *Grace Is a Pre-Existing Condition: Faith, Systems, and Mental Healthcare.* An ordained minister in the Christian Church (Disciples of Christ), he speaks and writes about the intersections among mental illness, mental health, and faith.

Rev. Gayle Fisher-Stewart is licensed in the Episcopal Diocese of Washington, DC, and is the editor of *Preaching Black Lives (Matter)*.

Dr. Virgil Fry is the Director Emeritus of Lifeline Chaplaincy in Houston, Texas.

Jennifer Grant is the author of several books for children and for adults, including *A Little Blue Bottle* and *Dimming the Day*.

Rev. Sonya Gravlee, a United Church of Christ pastor, serves as a chaplain at Ascension St. Vincent's East Hospital in Birmingham, Alabama.

Rev. Kelly Gregory is the Women and Children Clinical Chaplain at Presbyterian Hospital in Albuquerque, New Mexico.

Rev. Katherine K. Henderson is a healthcare chaplain and urban planner in Durham, North Carolina.

Rev. Laura D. Johnson is a minister in the United Church of Christ. She is a Palliative Care Chaplain at MedStar Washington Hospital Center in Washington, DC.

Rev. Hadley Kifner serves as the chaplain for the patients, families, and staff of the North Carolina Children's Hospital in Chapel Hill, North Carolina.

Rev. Arianne Braithwaite Lehn is the author of *Ash and Starlight: Prayers for the Chaos and Grace of Daily Life*. She is a team writer and editor for *Illustrated Ministry*.

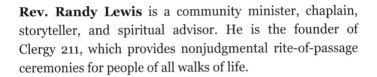

Rev. Randy Lewis is a community minister, chaplain, storyteller, and spiritual advisor. He is the founder of Clergy 211, which provides nonjudgmental rite-of-passage ceremonies for people of all walks of life.

Rev. Dr. Sarah Griffith Lund serves as senior pastor of First Congregational United Church of Christ of Indianapolis and as the UCC national staff Minister for Disabilities and Mental Health Justice. She is the author of *Blessed Are the Crazy: Breaking the Silence about Mental Illness, Family, and Church* and *Blessed Union: Breaking the Silence about Mental Illness and Marriage.*

Rev. Malcolm L. Marler is the Senior Director of Pastoral Care at UAB Medicine in Birmingham, Alabama. He has been a chaplain at UAB since March 1994.

Rev. Laura Martin serves as Associate Pastor at Rock Spring United Church of Christ in Arlington, Virginia.

Catherine McNiel is the author of *All Shall Be Well: Awakening to God's Presence in His Messy, Abundant World* and *Long Days of Small Things: Motherhood as a Spiritual Discipline.*

Dr. Catherine Meeks is Executive Director of the Absalom Jones Center for Racial Healing in Atlanta, Georgia.

Rev. Keith A. Menhinick is a progressive Baptist minister, trauma chaplain, and religion scholar passionate about questions of identity, body, trauma, and resilience.

Rev. Mandy Mizelle is a chaplain, minister, writer, retreat leader, and imperfection advocate who lives in Durham, North Carolina.

Rabbi Brian T. Nelson was ordained at HUC-JIR in 2016 and has been serving as a Chaplain Resident at UNC Health in Neurology and Palliative Care. He has a special interest in Mussar (value-centered character development) and blending progressive/liberal Judaism with contemporary mindfulness practices.

Rev. Kari Pellegrino is an ordained Minister of Word and Sacrament in the Presbyterian Church (USA) and serves as a staff chaplain at Saint Luke's North Hospital in Kansas City, Missouri.

Rev. Katherine Willis Pershey is one of the pastors at First Congregational Church of Western Springs, Illinois, a Chicago-area congregation affiliated with the United Church of Christ. She is the author of *Very Married: Field Notes on Love and Fidelity*.

Rev. Drew Phillips works as a staff chaplain at Ascension St. Vincent's Hospital in Birmingham, Alabama.

Claire Repsholdt is a student of Yale Divinity School and a chaplain at Yale New Haven Hospital in New Haven, Connecticut.

Jamie R. Rivera, LMT, CCAP, is a Certified Life Coach, executive assistant, and author in Fort Worth, Texas.

Rev. Kevin M. Roberts serves as the Director of Faith Relations for Habitat for Humanity of Greater Nashville, Tennessee.

Rev. Mishca R. Russell-Smith, MDiv, BCC, is a board-certified staff chaplain assigned to the emergency department at RUSH University Medical Center in Chicago, Illinois. He is an ordained itinerant elder of the African Methodist Episcopal Church and an associate minister on staff at Turner Memorial AME Church in the Bronzeville Community of Chicago.

Leenah Safi is a Muslim doctoral student at the Chicago Theological Seminary with special interests in the fields of practical and pastoral theology.

Rabbi Deborah Jill Schloss was ordained from the Jewish Theological Seminary in 1996 and is the rabbi of Temple Beth Tikvah in Houston, Texas, a board-certified hospital chaplain, and celebrant.

Rev. Ruth McMeekin Skjerseth is an Episcopalian and is active in retirement in outreach programs such as winter sheltering.

Rev. Traci Smith is a PC(USA) pastor and author of the Faithful Families series of books.

Rev. Sheila P. Spencer is a writer, educator, poet, spiritual director, preacher, mentor, author, and ordained Christian Church (Disciples of Christ) minister in Indianapolis, Indiana.

Rev. Martha Spong is a United Church of Christ pastor and clergy coach in Mechanicsburg, Pennsylvania. Her books include *Denial Is My Spiritual Practice (and Other Failures of Faith)* and *The Words of Her Mouth: Psalms for the Struggle.*

Rev. Jessica Stokes is on staff with the North Carolina Council of Churches, where she leads the statewide mental health advocacy efforts.

Rev. Ellen M. Swinford is an ACPE Certified Educator and an ordained minister in fellowship with the Unitarian Universalist Ministerial Association (UUMA). She is currently a member of the staff at the NIH Clinical Center in Bethesda, Maryland.

Rev. Ally Vertigan is an ordained minister with the United Church of Christ. She completed her training and began her career in chaplaincy at Rush University System for Health in Chicago.

Rev. Paula A. Wells is an ordained minister in the United Church of Christ, serving a church in Lexington, North Carolina. She also works as a lawyer, a business owner, and an end-of-life doula.

Rev. Ginny Wilder is a writer, a musician, and an Episcopal priest who serves as the rector of St. Anne's Episcopal Church in Winston Salem, North Carolina.

Rev. Mark Wingfield serves as executive director and publisher of Baptist News Global. He previously served seventeen years as associate pastor of Wilshire Baptist Church in Dallas, Texas.

Rev. Molly Brummett Wudel pastors at Emmaus Way Church in Durham, North Carolina.

Rev. Chelsea Brooke Yarborough is from Baltimore, Maryland, and is currently the visiting professor of liturgical studies at Wake Forest University School of Divinity. She is an ordained minister, poet, and Enneagram teacher and is pursuing her doctorate in homiletics and liturgics from Vanderbilt University.